Amigos de la granja / Farmyard Friends

LAS VACAS
COWS

Maddie Gibbs

Traducido por Eida de la Vega

PowerKiDS press.

New York

Dedicatoria: *Para mi padre, porque las vacas sí andan por ahí*
Dedication: *For my father, because cows do wander*

Published in 2015 by The Rosen Publishing Group, Inc.
29 East 21st Street, New York, NY 10010

First Edition

Editor: Caitie McAneney
Book Design: Katelyn Heinle
Spanish Translator: Eida de la Vega

Photo Credits: Cover, p. 1 smereka/Shutterstock.com; p. 5 steverts/Thinkstock.com; p. 6 Matthew Jacques/Shutterstock.com; pp. 9, 24 (calves) Fuse/Thinkstock.com; p. 10 David Maska/Shutterstock.com; pp. 13, 24 (horns) Leena Robinson/Shutterstock.com; p. 14 Robert Crow/Shutterstock.com; p. 17 Peter Bay/Shutterstock.com; p. 18 Dr Ajay Kumar Singh/Shutterstock.com; p. 21 Blend Images/Shutterstock.com; p. 22 Symbiot/Shutterstock.com; p. 24 (cheese) Sea Wave/Shutterstock.com; p. 24 (yogurt) tacar/Shutterstock.com.

Library of Congress Cataloging-in-Publication Data

Gibbs, Maddie, author.
 Cows = Las vacas / Maddie Gibbs.
     pages cm. — (Farmyard friends = Amigos de la granja)
Parallel title: Amigos de la granja.
In English and Spanish.
 Includes index.
 ISBN 978-1-4994-0265-0 (library binding)
1. Cows—Juvenile literature. I. Title.
SF239.5.G55 2015
636.2—dc23

Manufactured in the United States of America

CPSIA Compliance Information: Batch #CW15PK: For Further Information contact Rosen Publishing, New York, New York at 1-800-237-9932

CONTENIDO

CONTENTS

Las vacas viven en granjas.
Las crían para obtener
carne y leche.

Cows live on farms. People raise
them for meat and milk.

A las vacas de una granja a menudo se les dice ganado.

Cows on a farm are often called cattle.

Los machos se llaman toros.
Los bebés se llaman **terneros**.

Male cows are called bulls.
Baby cows are called **calves**.

El estómago de la vaca tiene
cuatro partes. Descompone
la comida que come.

A cow's stomach has four parts.
It breaks down the food a
cow eats.

Texas es famosa por su ganado Longhorn. Tienen **cuernos** largos.

Texas is famous for its longhorn cattle. They have long **horns**.

El ganado Angus es descornado. Esto significa que no tiene cuernos.

Angus cattle are polled. This means they have no horns.

El ganado de las tierras altas es muy peludo. Es de Escocia.

Highland cattle are furry.
They are from Scotland.

Las vacas Holstein son ganado lechero. Las crían por su leche.

Holsteins are dairy cattle. They are raised for their milk.

La gente toma leche de vaca.
Con la leche también hacemos
queso, **yogurt** y helado.

People drink cow milk. We also
make **cheese**, **yogurt**, and
ice cream from it.

Las vacas son animales provechosos. ¿Alguna vez has visto una vaca?

Cows are useful animals. Have you ever seen one?

PALABRAS QUE DEBES SABER
WORDS TO KNOW

(los) terneros
calves

(el) queso
cheese

(los) cuernos
horns

(el) yogurt
yogurt

ÍNDICE / INDEX

SITIOS DE INTERNET / WEBSITES

Due to the changing nature of Internet links, PowerKids Press has developed an online list of websites related to the subject of this book. This site is updated regularly. Please use this link to access the list: www.powerkidslinks.com/fmyd/cow